Shadow W

THIS JOURNAL BELONGS TO:

....

....

"Everyone carries a shadow, and the less it is embodied in the individual's conscious life, the blacker and denser it is. At all counts, it forms an unconscious snag, thwarting our most well-meant intentions."

— Carl Jung

Shadow work

What exactly is shadow work?

According to the psychologist Carl Gustav Jung the shadow is the unconscious or disowned side of your personality. It is born or created in childhood through the world view or beliefs parents project onto their kids.

How exactly does that work?

Imagine a boy who cries a lot and is very emotional. His father tells him to stop crying and to be a man. The boy learns that way, that this emotional part of him is not accepted and therefore must be something bad. The result is, that he begins to suppress this part of him in order to be accepted by his father.

With shadow work you can bring light to your shadow. It can show you these unconscious patterns that define your life and resolve them by making them conscious.

How This Book Help

We all have a shadow, a hidden part of our personality that lies discarded in the subconscious recesses of our mind. The shadow is unseen, but it subtly influences our behaviour and emotions, causing us to act without self awareness. Shadow work is the process of turning inwards for a journey of self discovery. Unlock the secrets of your psyche and form an unbreakable alliance with your shadow as you work through the exercises and prompts in this shadow work book.

Shadow work

In this journal u will find :

- 80 days Promts
- 8 Quotes
- 4 Blank Letters To ...
- 4 Pages for Notes
- 4 Mandala coloring pages

(It will help you relax and feel calm)

This shadow work journal walks you step by step through the shadow work process and aims to show you the unconscious patterns that define your experiences, thoughts and actions

Created By

Intuition Publishing

Shadow work prompts

Day 1: If present day me could talk to myself from 10 years ago, I would say....

Day 2: How I spend my days is how I'll spend my life. How do I feel about that ?

Day 3: My ideal day starts with....

Day 4: Getting triggered unexpectedly can be a positive thing because....

Day 5: When I think about my life in the present, I am most proud of

Day 6: Money and success are byproducts - not the goals - of my unique expression

Day 7: What are the current and recurring problems in my life? What would happen if I started viewing problems as opportunities?

Day 8: What I want and what I need are not always the same

Day 9: A rejection can point me in the right direction. An example of this in my life is

Day 10: When I think about my future, I am most excited about

Day 11: If I'm feeling stressed, it means I am resisting something

Day 12: If part of my consciousness is not awake, something in my body will suffer for it

Day 13: I can't fix, change or improve anyone. I can only inspire. How can I lead by example?

Day 14: True wellness involves fitness. And true fitness never compromises wellness

Day 15: The opposite of depression is not happiness. It's purpose

Day 16: Do I actively listen from my heart? Or do I analyse with my mind? Which is more likely to help and heal others? Why ?

Day 17: Mindfulness turns habits into rituals and ceremonies

Day 18: I feel happy and confident in my body when I ....

Day 19: I really want recognition for ....

Day 20: I really wish others understood this about me ....

Day 21: What does 'freedom' mean to me? What does it feel like ?

Shadow work prompts

Day 22: My ideal week feels like?

Day 23: I felt especially valued and loved when ....

Day 24: Am I a spiritual person?

Day 25: When I think about my future, I am most afraid of ....

Day 26: Do I project aspects of myself onto others?

Day 27: When I think about my future, I am most excited about ....

Day 28: Who is my 'highest self?

Day 29: The way I define my values over the last few years has changed ....

Day 30: I feel the most energised when ....

Day 31: Make a list of words and phrases which describe how you feel about your early childhood

Day 32: Which option currently looks a lot more attractive than it probably is in reality? Be honest

Day 33: Think about the three most important relationships in your life right now. To what extent are you being authentic in each of them? Go deep. Get clear

Day 34: Is it important to feel physically attractive? Why or why not?

Day 35: What's your biggest block when it comes to living life on your own terms?

Day 36: What drives you to be better at the moment?

Day 37: How did you protect your ego today?

Day 38: How important is it to have a close connection to nature?

Day 39: If money was no object, who would you refuse to offer financial help to and why?

Day 40: Is empathy ever a negative thing? Why or why not?

Day 41: What is the true value of art for the purposes of healing?

Day 42: Which rule do you want to break more than any other?

Day 43: What is enchantment? When was the last time you were enchanted?

Shadow work prompts

Day 44: How can you be of service in a meaningful way at this point?

Day 45: How often do you judge people on their looks?

Day 46: Which qualities are the most important in a parent?

Day 47: Who do you pity the most right now and why?

Day 48: If you could make a film about one short period of your life so far, which time would you choose and why?

Day 49: When was the last time you felt totally exposed and vulnerable?

Day 50: Which responsibility can you drop right now for the sake of your own happiness?

Day 51: What is the purpose of anger?

Day 52: Promises are sometimes broken. How has this truth been evident in your own life?

Day 53: Do you hold all people in your life to the same standards more or less? Or do you tend to make excuses for key people? If so, who and on what grounds?

Day 54: Change is a fact of life. In what way does this tend to scare you?

Day 55: What is the relationship between destruction and success?

Day 56: What could you be more grateful for?

Day 57: When was the last time you let someone mess with your mood?

Day 58: What will your next big adventure look like?

Day 59: Which relationship needs to be eliminated?

Day 60: How would you use your wisdom and experience to help someone cope with heartbreak?

Day 61: When was the last time you were surprised by your emotional reaction to something someone said?

Day 62: Which song lyrics represent your current situation and why?

Day 63: How many different forms of love have you directly experienced?

Shadow work prompts

Day 64: When was the last time you were awe-inspired ?

Day 65: What does the word 'grace' make you think of? How do you practice and/or embody grace in your life ?

Day 66: Whose perception seems to be clashing violently with yours right now and how so ?

Day 67: Are you secretly in possession of something which could help other people? Why are you keeping it to yourself ?

Day 68: Which character traits tend to make you feel a sense of superiority over the person displaying them ?

Day 69: Do you often feel the need to apologise for following your instincts and doing your own thing? Explore your answer in-depth

Day 70: What are you still waiting for ?

Day 71: Do you tend to feel trapped and confused when you have too many options to choose from? Why or why not? Why do you think so many people feel trapped by an abundance of options ?

Day 72: What does your conduct in the outside world say about who you are as a person ?

Day 73: What really disgusts you right now? Make a list

Day 74: What does the word 'purity' make you think of ?

Day 75: Do you think there is an opportunity for major awakening and realisation this year? If not, why not? If so, in what sense ?

Day 76: Can human beings really 'lose their innocence'? Go deep with this

Day 77: Which question would you really like an answer to right now ?

Day 78: If you wanted to find a place of sanctuary right now, where would you go and why

Day 79: Where abouts are you currently feeling impatient and frustrated ?

Day 80: Which fear could you make more effort to overcome ?

Day 1

If present day me could talk to myself from 10 years ago, I would say ...

Notes

Appreciate 3 Things About Yourself and Your life Today

1-
2-
3-

Any Triggers Today Who & Why ?

Day 2

How I spend my days is how I'll spend my life. How do I feel about that?

Notes

Appreciate 3 Things About Yourself and Your life Today

1-
2-
3-

Any Triggers Today Who & Why ?

Day 3

My ideal day starts with....

Notes

Appreciate 3 Things About Yourself and Your life Today

1 -
2 -
3 -

Any Triggers Today Who & Why ?

Day 4

Getting triggered unexpectedly can be a positive thing because....

Notes

Appreciate 3 Things About Yourself and Your life Today

1-
2-
3-

Any Triggers Today Who & Why ?

Day 5

When I think about my life in the present, I am most proud of

Notes

Appreciate 3 Things About Yourself and Your life Today

1-
2-
3-

Any Triggers Today Who & Why ?

Day 6

Money and success are byproducts - not the goals - of my unique expression ...

Notes

Appreciate 3 Things About Yourself and Your life Today

1-
2-
3-

Any Triggers Today Who & Why ?

Day 7

What are the current and recurring problems in my life ? What would happen if I started viewing problems as opportunities ?

Notes

Appreciate 3 Things About Yourself and Your life Today

1-
2-
3-

Any Triggers Today Who & Why ?

Day 8

What I want and what I need are not always the same ...

Notes

Appreciate 3 Things About Yourself and Your life Today

1-
2-
3-

Any Triggers Today Who & Why ?

Day 9

A rejection can point me in the right direction. An example of this in my life is ...

Notes

Appreciate 3 Things About Yourself and Your life Today

1-
2-
3-

Any Triggers Today Who & Why ?

Day 10

When I think about my future, I am most excited about ...

Notes

Appreciate 3 Things About Yourself and Your life Today

1-
2-
3-

Any Triggers Today Who & Why ?

Day 11

If I'm feeling stressed, it means I am resisting something

Notes

Appreciate 3 Things About Yourself and Your life Today

1 -
2 -
3 -

Any Triggers Today Who & Why ?

Day 12

If part of my consciousness is not awake, something in my body will suffer for it

Notes

Appreciate 3 Things About Yourself and Your life Today

1-
2-
3-

Any Triggers Today Who & Why ?

Day 13

I can't fix, change or improve anyone. I can only inspire. How can I lead by example?

Notes

Appreciate 3 Things About Yourself and Your life Today

1-
2-
3-

Any Triggers Today Who & Why?

Day 14

True wellness involves fitness. And true fitness never compromises wellness

Notes

Appreciate 3 Things About Yourself and Your life Today

1-
2-
3-

Any Triggers Today Who & Why ?

Day 15

The opposite of depression is not happiness. It's purpose

Notes

Appreciate 3 Things About Yourself and Your life Today

1-
2-
3-

Any Triggers Today Who & Why ?

Day 16

Do I actively listen from my heart? Or do I analyse with my mind? Which is more likely to help and heal others? Why?

Notes

Appreciate 3 Things About Yourself and Your life Today

1-
2-
3-

Any Triggers Today Who & Why?

Day 17

Mindfulness turns habits into rituals and ceremonies

Notes

Appreciate 3 Things About Yourself and Your life Today

1-
2-
3-

Any Triggers Today Who & Why ?

Day 18

I feel happy and confident in my body when I ...

Notes

Appreciate 3 Things About Yourself and Your life Today

1-
2-
3-

Any Triggers Today Who & Why ?

Day 19

I really want recognition for ...

Notes

Appreciate 3 Things About Yourself and Your life Today

1-
2-
3-

Any Triggers Today Who & Why ?

Day 20

I really wish others understood this about me ...

Notes

Appreciate 3 Things About Yourself and Your life Today

1-
2-
3-

Any Triggers Today Who & Why ?

Day 21

What does 'freedom' mean to me? What does it feel like?

Notes

Appreciate 3 Things About Yourself and Your life Today

1 -
2 -
3 -

Any Triggers Today Who & Why?

Day 22

My ideal week feels like ?

Notes

Appreciate 3 Things About Yourself and Your life Today

1-
2-
3-

Any Triggers Today Who & Why ?

Day 23

I felt especially valued and loved when ...

Notes

Appreciate 3 Things About Yourself and Your life Today

1-
2-
3-

Any Triggers Today Who & Why ?

Day 24

Am I a spiritual person?

Notes

Appreciate 3 Things About Yourself and Your life Today

1-
2-
3-

Any Triggers Today Who & Why?

Day 25

When I think about my future, I am most afraid of ....

Notes

Appreciate 3 Things About Yourself and Your life Today

1-
2-
3-

Any Triggers Today Who & Why ?

Day 26

Do I project aspects of myself onto others?

Notes

Appreciate 3 Things About Yourself and Your life Today

1-
2-
3-

Any Triggers Today Who & Why?

Day 27

When I think about my future, I am most excited about ....

Notes

Appreciate 3 Things About Yourself and Your life Today

1-
2-
3-

Any Triggers Today Who & Why ?

Day 28
Who is my 'highest self ?

Notes

Appreciate 3 Things About Yourself and Your life Today

1 -
2 -
3 -

Any Triggers Today Who & Why ?

Day 29

The way I define my values over the last few years has changed ...

Notes _____

_____
_____
_____
_____
_____
_____
_____
_____
_____
_____
_____
_____
_____
_____
_____
_____

Appreciate 3 Things About Yourself and Your life Today

1- _____
2- _____
3- _____

Any Triggers Today Who & Why ?

_____
_____
_____

Day 30

I feel the most energised when ...

Notes

Appreciate 3 Things About Yourself and Your life Today

1-
2-
3-

Any Triggers Today Who & Why ?

Day 31

Make a list of words and phrases which describe how you feel about your early childhood ...

Notes

Appreciate 3 Things About Yourself and Your life Today

1-
2-
3-

Any Triggers Today Who & Why ?

Day 32

Which option currently looks a lot more attractive than it probably is in reality? Be honest

Notes

Appreciate 3 Things About Yourself and Your life Today

1-
2-
3-

Any Triggers Today Who & Why?

Day 33

Think about the three most important relationships in your life right now. To what extent are you being authentic in each of them? Go deep. Get clear

Notes

Appreciate 3 Things About Yourself and Your life Today

1-
2-
3-

Any Triggers Today Who & Why ?

Day 34

Is it important to feel physically attractive? Why or why not?

Notes

Appreciate 3 Things About Yourself and Your life Today

1-
2-
3-

Any Triggers Today Who & Why?

Day 35

What's your biggest block when it comes to living life on your own terms ?

Notes

Appreciate 3 Things About Yourself and Your life Today

1 -
2 -
3 -

Any Triggers Today Who & Why ?

Day 36

What drives you to be better at the moment?

Notes

Appreciate 3 Things About Yourself and Your life Today

1-
2-
3-

Any Triggers Today Who & Why?

Day 37

How did you protect your ego today ?

Notes

Appreciate 3 Things About Yourself and Your life Today

1-
2-
3-

Any Triggers Today Who & Why ?

Day 38

How important is it to have a close connection to nature ?

Notes

Appreciate 3 Things About Yourself and Your life Today

1-
2-
3-

Any Triggers Today Who & Why ?

Day 39

If money was no object, who would you refuse to offer financial help to and why ?

Notes

Appreciate 3 Things About Yourself and Your life Today

1-
2-
3-

Any Triggers Today Who & Why ?

Day 40

Is empathy ever a negative thing? Why or why not?

Notes

Appreciate 3 Things About Yourself and Your life Today

1-
2-
3-

Any Triggers Today Who & Why?

Day 41

What is the true value of art for the purposes of healing ?

Notes

Appreciate 3 Things About Yourself and Your life Today

1 -
2 -
3 -

Any Triggers Today Who & Why ?

Day 42

Which rule do you want to break more than any other?

Notes

Appreciate 3 Things About Yourself and Your life Today

1-
2-
3-

Any Triggers Today Who & Why?

Day 43

What is enchantment ? When was the last time you were enchanted ?

Notes

Appreciate 3 Things About Yourself and Your life Today

1-
2-
3-

Any Triggers Today Who & Why ?

Day 44

How can you be of service in a meaningful way at this point?

Notes

Appreciate 3 Things About Yourself and Your life Today

1-
2-
3-

Any Triggers Today Who & Why?

Day 45

How often do you judge people on their looks ?

Notes

Appreciate 3 Things About Yourself and Your life Today

1 -
2 -
3 -

Any Triggers Today Who & Why ?

Day 46

Which qualities are the most important in a parent ?

Notes

Appreciate 3 Things About Yourself and Your life Today

1-
2-
3-

Any Triggers Today Who & Why ?

Day 47

Who do you pity the most right now and why ?

Notes

Appreciate 3 Things About Yourself and Your life Today

1-
2-
3-

Any Triggers Today Who & Why ?

Day 48

If you could make a film about one short period of your life so far, which time would you choose and why?

Notes

Appreciate 3 Things About Yourself and Your life Today

1-
2-
3-

Any Triggers Today Who & Why?

# Day 49

When was the last time you felt totally exposed and vulnerable ?

Notes

Appreciate 3 Things About Yourself and Your life Today

1 -
2 -
3 -

Any Triggers Today Who & Why ?

Day 50

Which responsibility can you drop right now for the sake of your own happiness ?

Notes

Appreciate 3 Things About Yourself and Your life Today

1-
2-
3-

Any Triggers Today Who & Why ?

Day 51

What is the purpose of anger?

Notes

Appreciate 3 Things About Yourself and Your life Today

1-
2-
3-

Any Triggers Today Who & Why?

Day 52

Promises are sometimes broken. How has this truth been evident in your own life?

Notes

Appreciate 3 Things About Yourself and Your life Today

1-
2-
3-

Any Triggers Today Who & Why?

Day 53

Do you hold all people in your life to the same standards more or less ? Or do you tend to make excuses for key people ? If so, who and on what grounds ?

Notes

Appreciate 3 Things About Yourself and Your life Today

1-
2-
3-

Any Triggers Today Who & Why ?

Day 54

Change is a fact of life. In what way does this tend to scare you ?

Notes _____

Appreciate 3 Things About Yourself and Your life Today

1-
2-
3-

Any Triggers Today Who & Why ?

Day 55

What is the relationship between destruction and success ?

Notes

Appreciate 3 Things About Yourself and Your life Today

1-
2-
3-

Any Triggers Today Who & Why ?

Day 56
What could you be more grateful for ?

Notes

Appreciate 3 Things About Yourself and Your life Today

1-
2-
3-

Any Triggers Today Who & Why ?

Day 57

When was the last time you let someone mess with your mood?

Notes

Appreciate 3 Things About Yourself and Your life Today

1 -
2 -
3 -

Any Triggers Today Who & Why?

Day 58

What will your next big adventure look like ?

Notes

Appreciate 3 Things About Yourself and Your life Today

1 -
2 -
3 -

Any Triggers Today Who & Why ?

Day 59

Which relationship needs to be eliminated ?

Notes

Appreciate 3 Things About Yourself and Your life Today

1-
2-
3-

Any Triggers Today Who & Why ?

Day 60

How would you use your wisdom and experience to help someone cope with heartbreak ?

Notes

Appreciate 3 Things About Yourself and Your life Today

1-
2-
3-

Any Triggers Today Who & Why ?

Day 61

When was the last time you were surprised by your emotional reaction to something someone said ?

Notes

Appreciate 3 Things About Yourself and Your life Today

1-
2-
3-

Any Triggers Today Who & Why ?

Day 62

Which song lyrics represent your current situation and why?

Notes

Appreciate 3 Things About Yourself and Your life Today

1-
2-
3-

Any Triggers Today Who & Why?

Day 63

How many different forms of love have you directly experienced?

Notes

Appreciate 3 Things About Yourself and Your life Today

1-
2-
3-

Any Triggers Today Who & Why?

Day 64

When was the last time you were awe-inspired ?

Notes _____

Appreciate 3 Things About Yourself and Your life Today

1-
2-
3-

Any Triggers Today Who & Why ?

Day 65

What does the word 'grace' make you think of? How do you practice and/or embody grace in your life?

Notes

Appreciate 3 Things About Yourself and Your life Today

1-
2-
3-

Any Triggers Today Who & Why?

Day 66

Whose perception seems to be clashing violently with yours right now and how so?

Notes

Appreciate 3 Things About Yourself and Your life Today

1-
2-
3-

Any Triggers Today Who & Why?

Day 67

Are you secretly in possession of something which could help other people? Why are you keeping it to yourself?

Notes

Appreciate 3 Things About Yourself and Your life Today

1-
2-
3-

Any Triggers Today Who & Why?

Day 68

Which character traits tend to make you feel a sense of superiority over the person displaying them ?

Notes

Appreciate 3 Things About Yourself and Your life Today

1-
2-
3-

Any Triggers Today Who & Why ?

Day 69

Do you often feel the need to apologise for following your instincts and doing your own thing? Explore your answer in-depth

Notes

Appreciate 3 Things About Yourself and Your life Today

1-
2-
3-

Any Triggers Today Who & Why ?

Day 70

What are you still waiting for ?

Notes

Appreciate 3 Things About Yourself and Your life Today

1-
2-
3-

Any Triggers Today Who & Why ?

Day 71

Do you tend to feel trapped and confused when you have too many options to choose from? Why or why not? Why do you think so many people feel trapped by an abundance of options?

Notes

Appreciate 3 Things About Yourself and Your Life Today

1-
2-
3-

Any Triggers Today Who & Why?

Day 72

What does your conduct in the outside world say about who you are as a person ?

Notes

Appreciate 3 Things About Yourself and Your life Today

1-
2-
3-

Any Triggers Today Who & Why ?

Day 73

What really disgusts you right now? Make a list

Notes

Appreciate 3 Things About Yourself and Your life Today

1 -
2 -
3 -

Any Triggers Today Who & Why?

Day 74

What does the word 'purity' make you think of ?

Notes

Appreciate 3 Things About Yourself and Your life Today

1-
2-
3-

Any Triggers Today Who & Why ?

Day 75

Do you think there is an opportunity for major awakening and realisation this year? If not, why not? If so, in what sense?

Notes

Appreciate 3 Things About Yourself and Your life Today

1 -
2 -
3 -

Any Triggers Today Who & Why ?

Day 76

Can human beings really 'lose their innocence'? Go deep with this

Notes

Appreciate 3 Things About Yourself and Your life Today

1-
2-
3-

Any Triggers Today Who & Why ?

Day 77

Which question would you really like an answer to right now ?

Notes

Appreciate 3 Things About Yourself and Your life Today

1-
2-
3-

Any Triggers Today Who & Why ?

Day 78

If you wanted to find a place of sanctuary right now, where would you go and why

Notes

Appreciate 3 Things About Yourself and Your life Today

1-
2-
3-

Any Triggers Today Who & Why ?

Day 79

Where abouts are you currently feeling impatient and frustrated?

Notes _____

_____
_____
_____
_____
_____
_____
_____
_____
_____
_____
_____
_____
_____
_____
_____
_____
_____

Appreciate 3 Things About Yourself and Your life Today

1- _____
2- _____
3- _____

Any Triggers Today Who & Why?

_____
_____
_____

Day 80

Which fear could you make more effort to overcome ?

Notes

Appreciate 3 Things About Yourself and Your life Today

1-
2-
3-

Any Triggers Today Who & Why ?

> "When we are aware of our weaknesses or negative tendencies, we open the opportunity to work on them." — Djuna Barnes

"The shadow escapes from the body like an animal we had been sheltering."
—Gilles Deleuze

"Every pain, addiction, anguish, longing, depression, anger or fear is an orphaned part of us seeking joy, some disowned shadow wanting to return to the light and home of ourselves."
— Jacob Nordby

"Believing you are good is like believing in the half moon."
—Thomas Lloyd Qualls

"Your Shadow is a dark omen, a powerful teacher that reveals to you the places in your life where you are energetically blocked. When you continue to ignore these signs, you perpetuate the cycle of your suffering."
— Mateo Sol

"The shadow is needed now more than ever. We heal the world when we heal ourselves, and hope shines brightest when it illuminates the dark."
—Sasha Graham

"Your Shadow is all of the things, 'positive' and 'negative', that you've denied about yourself and hidden beneath the surface of the mask you forgot that you're wearing."
— Oli Anderson

"The shadow is a moral problem that challenges the whole ego-personality, for no one can become conscious of the shadow without considerable moral effort. To become conscious of it involves recognizing the dark aspects of the personality as present and real. This act is the essential condition for any kind of self-knowledge."
— Carl Jung

This Letter To

This Letter To

This Letter To

This Letter To

Reflections

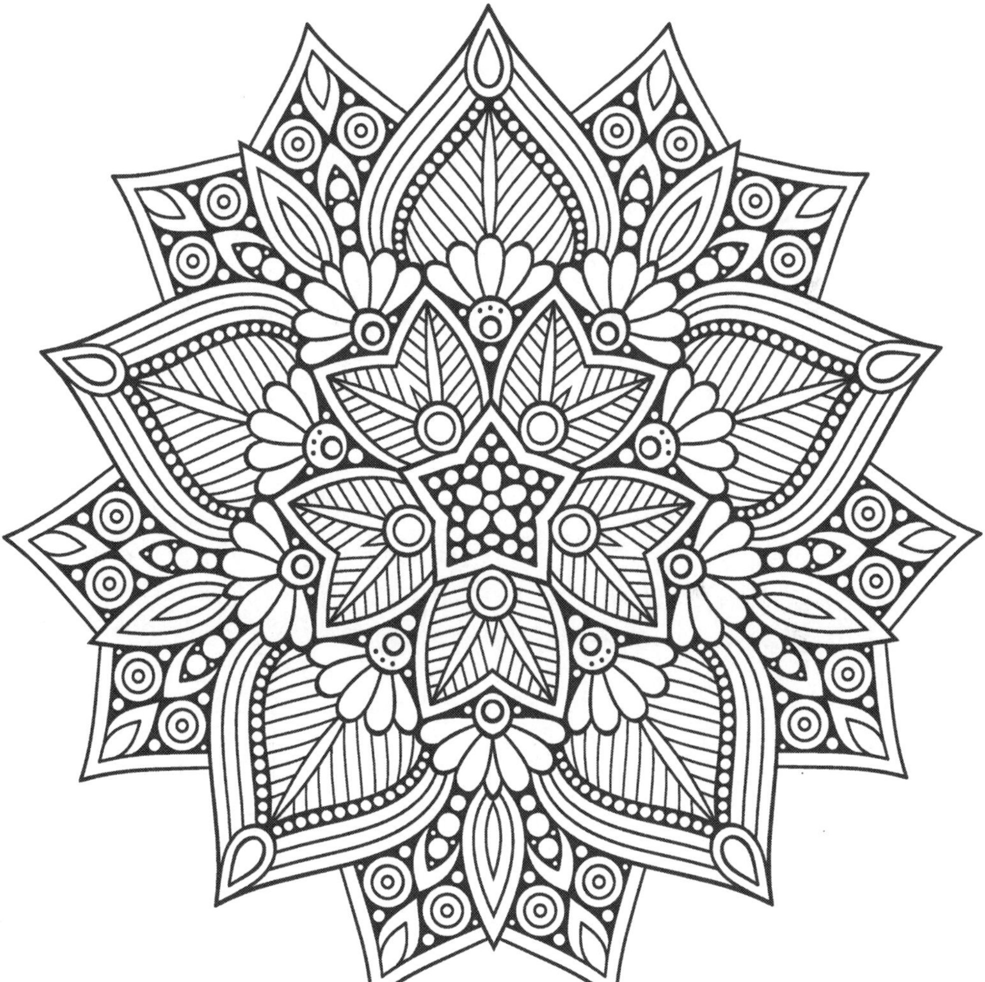

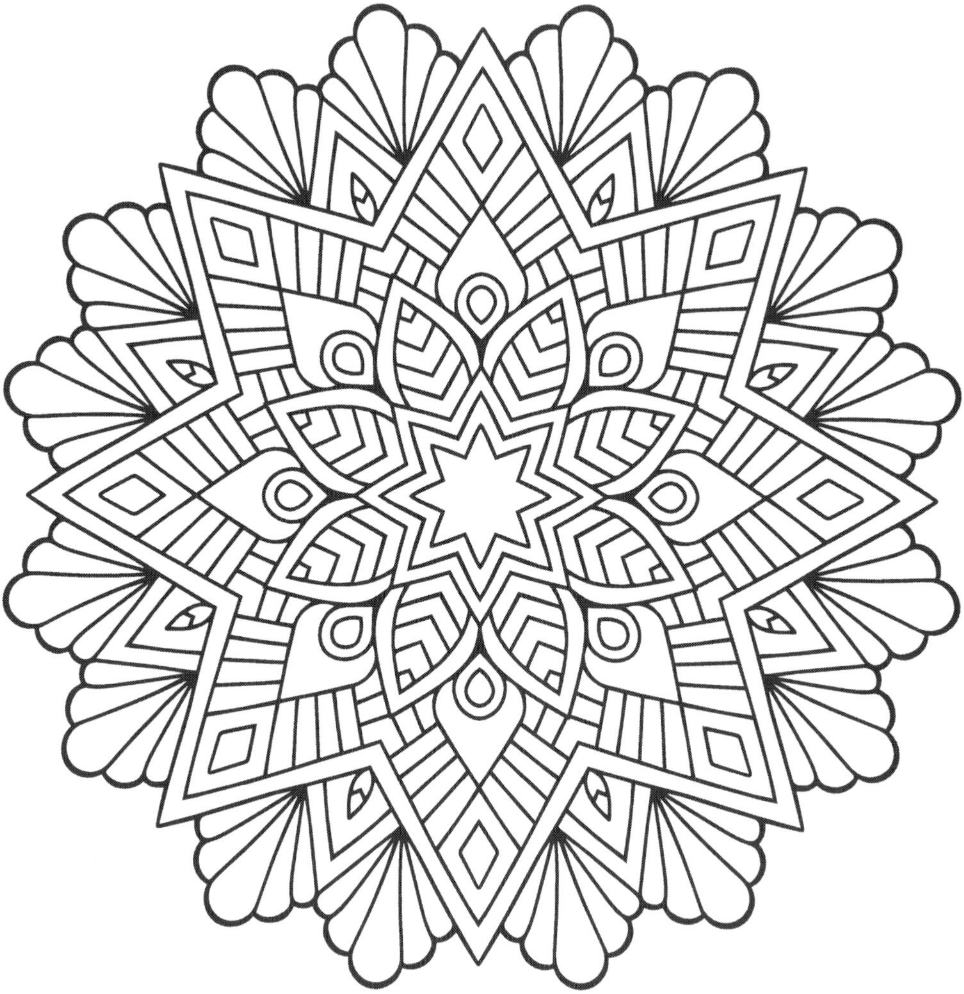

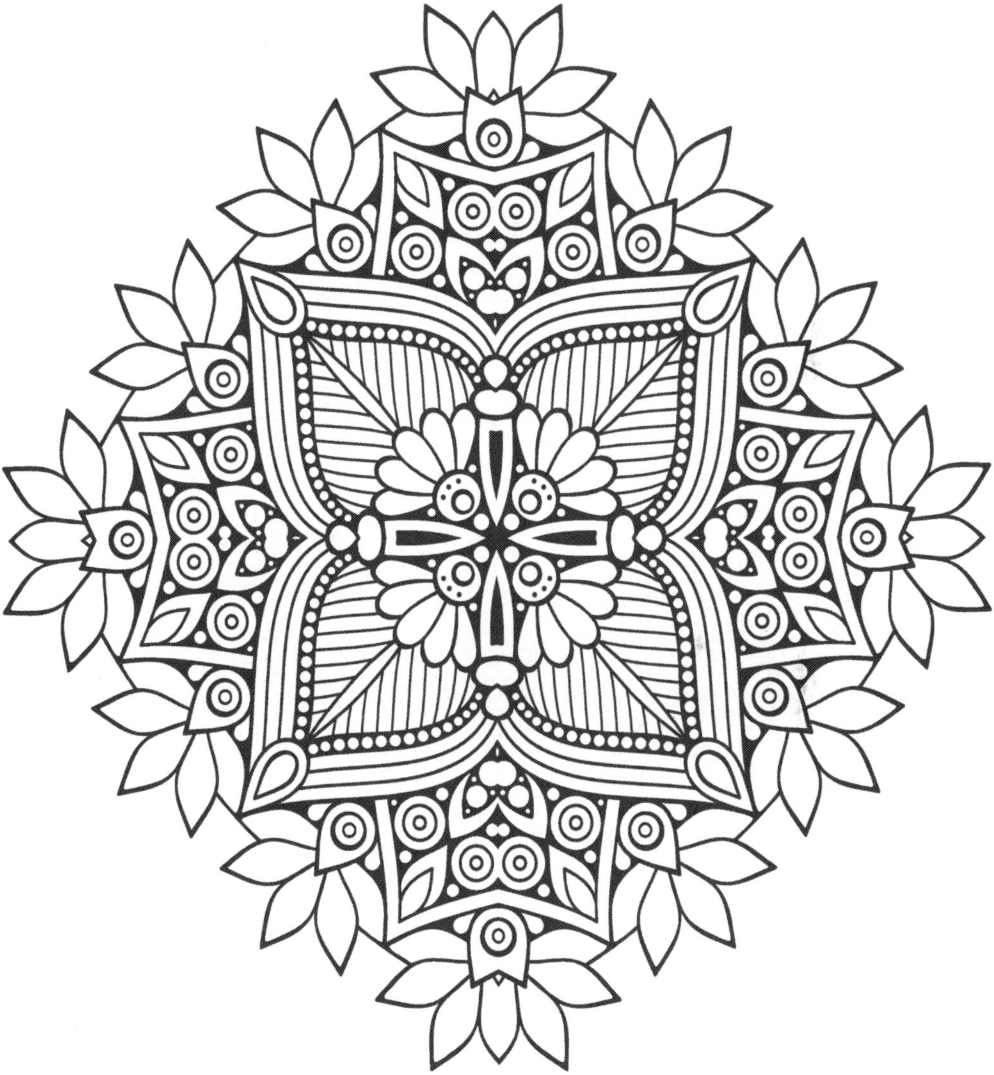

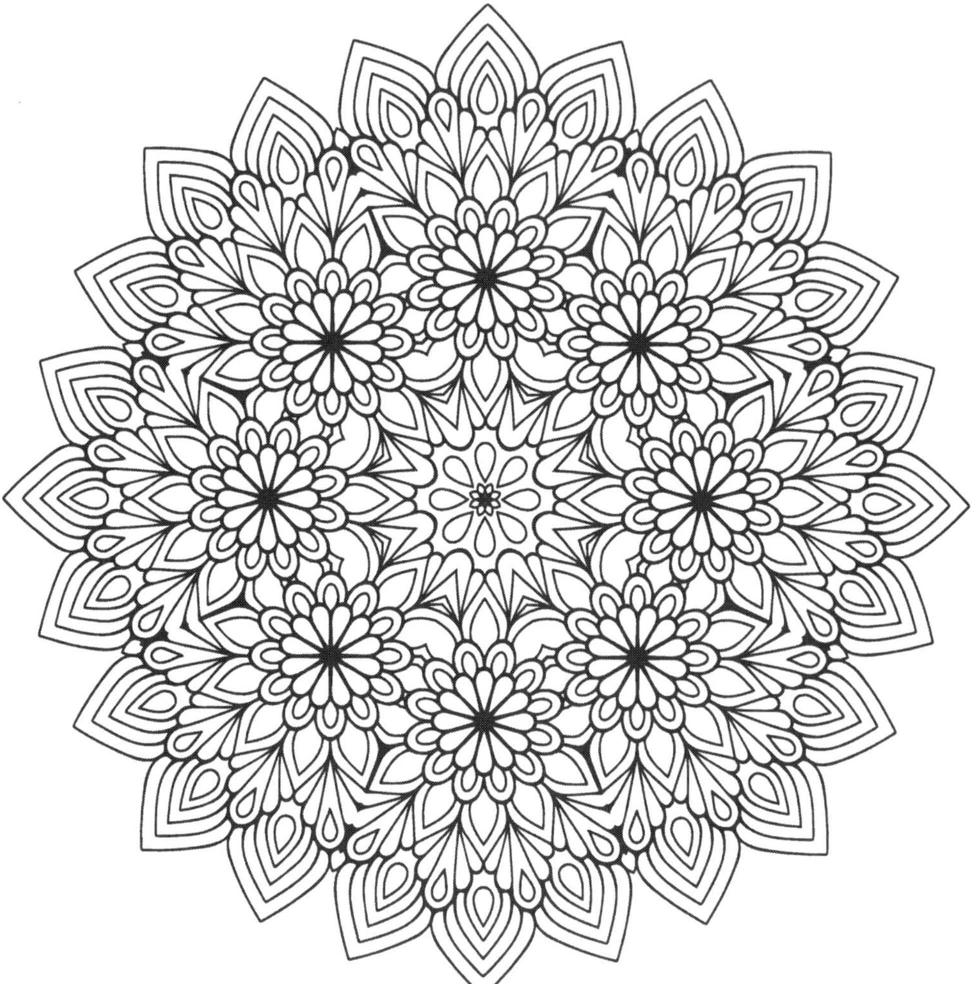

Thank you

For completing our journal, You can get more great versions on our Amazon Shop [Intuition Publishing]
If you like this journal please give us a good review why not a picture with the book maybe it will incourage other to have the same experience with small action

INTUITION
PUBLISHING

Made in the USA
Middletown, DE
30 October 2021